Beyond Service Lies the Experience
Wisdom Edition

Taking your Business and Marketing to the mind-blowing, customer-getting, client-keeping, insane-profit-generating level that the instant-gratification, fun-loving, got-to-have-it-right-now generation demands.

David B. Whitfield

Power in Numbers Publishing
Houston, Texas

Published in the United States of America: revision March 18, 2011

Power In Numbers Publishing

ISBN-13: 978-0615466002 (Custom)

ISBN-10: 0615466001

BISAC: Business & Economics / Advertising & Promotion

Dedication

Thank you to Kevin Caddenhead, who gave me my first professional marketing position; to Jesse Chaluh, who raised my standard of living; and to David Oakes, whose trust allowed my moonlighting to grow into the business that spawned this book.

To my lovely wife, Cherish, who endured all the hardships of being married to a dreamer. Thank you.

Before we jump into the experience let me share with you…

Wisdom for Business from God and man…
a preview

For me my faith is part of everything I do, so frankly I am surprised it took me this long to start writing this book.   As I write I will share some of the topics as blog post for everyone. For my coaching clients, I will have even more pre-production content. I hope to have the Wisdom for Business from God and man available online and in stores by January 2012. Until them please enjoy this preview.

May you achieve success as you define it!

The Wisdom of Achievement

Achievement is an extremely tricky topic; how each reader defines it will be different. For the purpose of this article we will say achievement is reaching the business goal you have set without sacrificing family or faith to do it. I have often heard people say I would have succeeded except for "blank". I generally ask what they did after they corrected "blank". They look at me strangely and say nothing, I failed. I have always told anyone who came to me for advice that,"You only fail when you cease to strive for your desired result."

Anything else is a setback, minor or major, but only a setback all the same. Who gets credit for your achievements is equally important. I recall someone saying, "It's amazing how much you can get done if no one cares who gets the credit." Because I recognize the importance of that concept I have *Phil. 2:2-4, ²then make my joy complete by being like-minded, having the same love, being one in spirit and purpose. ³Do nothing out of selfish ambition or vain conceit, but in humility consider others better than yourselves. ⁴Each of you should look not only to your own interests, but also to the interests of others.*, printed and posted where I can see it whenever I sit down to work. Set goals, work hard, expect and overcome setback and give glory to God and those who help you succeed and you will find achievement!

From Man:

I don't care how much power, brilliance or energy you have, if you don't harness it and focus it on a specific target, and hold it there you're never going to accomplish as much as your ability warrants.
Zig Ziglar

If you have a task to perform and are vitally interested in it, excited and challenged by it, then you will exert maximum energy. But in the excitement, the pain of fatigue dissipates, and the exuberance of what you hope to achieve overcomes the weariness. Jimmy Carter

From God:

1 Kings 10:6-9

[6] She said to the king, "The report I heard in my own country about your achievements and your wisdom is true. [7] But I did not believe these things until I came and saw with my own eyes. Indeed, not even half was told me; in wisdom and wealth you have far exceeded the report I heard. [8] How happy your men must be! How happy your officials, who continually stand before you and hear your wisdom! [9] Praise be to the LORD your God, who has delighted in you and placed you on the throne of Israel. Because of the LORD's eternal love for Israel, he has made you king, to maintain justice and righteousness."

Matthew 7:12-14 (MSG)

"Here is a simple, rule-of-thumb guide for behavior: Ask yourself what you want people to do for you, then grab the initiative and do it for them. Add up God's Law and Prophets and this is what you get. Don't look for shortcuts to God. The market is flooded with surefire, easygoing formulas for a successful life that can be practiced in your spare time. Don't fall for that stuff, even though crowds of people do. The way to life—to God!—is vigorous and requires total attention.

The Wisdom of Accountability

Business owners small and large must have accountability as one of their highest priorities. We must hold everyone involved with our business accountable, but what does that mean? First and foremost we must hold ourselves to the highest standards of honesty, integrity. Only then can we set expectations and realistically expect others to follow.

As a leader you must recognize what someone is responsible for. Job descriptions are a good way of setting the basic expectations. Second, make sure they have the skills to do what you want to hold the accountable for. Even the best intentions without the skills will not achieve the desired results. Lastly follow up. If the job is not being done give it to someone who can get it done.

You are accountable to yourself and your clients. You are the boss it is ultimately your responsibility!

From Man:

...leaders who do not hold their people accountable to a set standard are, in effect, thieves and liars. Thieves because they are stealing from the stockholder who pays them to hold people accountable, and liars because they pretend that everything is OK with their people when in fact everything is not OK. - <u>James C. Hunter, The Servant</u>

"The ancient Romans had a tradition: whenever one of their engineers constructed an arch, as the capstone was hoisted into place, the engineer assumed accountability for his work in the most profound way possible: he stood under the arch - ." <u>Michael Armstrong</u>

From God:

2 Kings 12

[4] Joash said to the priests, "Collect all the money that is brought as sacred offerings to the temple of the LORD—the money collected in the census, the money received from personal vows and the money brought voluntarily to the temple. [5] Let every priest receive the money from one of the treasurers, then use it to repair whatever damage is found in the temple."

[6] But by the twenty-third year of King Joash the priests still had not repaired the temple. [7] Therefore King Joash summoned Jehoiada the priest and the other priests and asked them, "Why aren't you repairing the damage done to the temple? Take no more money from your treasurers, but hand it over for repairing the temple." [8] The priests agreed that they would not collect any more money from the people and that they would not repair the temple themselves.

[11] ...they gave the money to the men appointed to supervise the work on the temple. With it they paid those who worked on the temple of the LORD—the carpenters and builders, [12] the masons and stonecutters. They purchased timber and blocks of dressed stone for the repair of the temple of the LORD, and met all the other expenses of restoring the temple.

The Wisdom of Persistence

In business we often find ourselves having to overcome obstacles of all kinds. These issues may be supply or labor issues or simply the seemingly infinite time between customers or clients. Often times, complications are beyond our control. They can be caused by the actions of others, a down turn in the economy or a myriad of others possibilities. If we have prepared, planed and are working diligently then our only recourse is persistence and prayer.

From man:

"Success is almost totally dependent upon drive and persistence. The extra energy required to make another effort or try another approach is the secret of winning." **--Dennis Waitley, The Dragon and the Eagle**

"The majority of men meet with failure because of their lack of persistence in creating new plans to take the place of those which fail." **--Napoleon Hill, Think and Grow Rich**

From God:

Luke 18:1-8

[1]Then Jesus told his disciples a parable to show them that they should always pray and not give up. [2]He said: "In a certain town there was a judge who neither feared God nor cared about men. [3]And there was a widow in that town who kept coming to him with the plea, 'Grant me justice against my adversary.'

[4]"For some time he refused. But finally he said to himself, 'Even though I don't fear God or care about men, [5]yet because this widow keeps bothering me, I will see that she gets justice, so that she won't eventually wear me out with her coming!' "

[6]And the Lord said, "Listen to what the unjust judge says. [7]And will not God bring about justice for his chosen ones, who cry out to him day and night? Will he keep putting them off? [8]I tell you, he will see that they get justice, and quickly. However, when the Son of Man comes, will he find faith on the earth?"

The Wisdom of Preparation

"Luck is where opportunity and preparation meet." I do not generally begin with a quote but this one so defines my thoughts I had to lead with it. In business and life we have a choice to prepare or take things as they come. Perhaps when we were teenagers we could choose the second option. As business people we must plan our days to maximize productivity, our quarter to insure growth and long term plans to offer direction and a vision. As a rule, I plan very detailed tasks for the day and more generally for the week with some specifics. For months and years I create a frame work with specific goals, but only general strategies, because too many things are guaranteed to change to waste time with exact details. A vision for the future you wish to create will serve well enough, provided you add the appropriated detail when years become months, months become weeks and weeks become days.

From Man:

Opportunity is a haughty goddess who wastes no time with those who are   unprepared.
-George Clason Richest Man in Babylon

Victorious warriors win first and then go to war, while defeated warriors go to war first and then seek to win. -Sun Tzu The Art of War

From God:

Matthew 25 1-13

[1] "Here is what the kingdom of heaven will be like at that time. Ten bridesmaids took their lamps and went out to meet the groom. [2] Five of them were foolish. Five were wise. [3] The foolish ones took their lamps but didn't take any olive oil with them. [4] The wise ones took oil in jars along with their lamps. [5] The groom did not come for a long time. So the bridesmaids all grew tired and fell asleep.

[6] "At midnight someone cried out, 'Here's the groom! Come out to meet him!' [7] "Then all the bridesmaids woke up and got their lamps ready. [8] The foolish ones said to the wise ones, 'Give us some of your oil. Our lamps are going out.' [9] " 'No,' they replied. 'There may not be enough for all of us. Instead, go to those who sell oil. Buy some for yourselves.'

[10] "So they went to buy the oil. But while they were on their way, the groom arrived. The bridesmaids who were ready went in with him to the wedding dinner. Then the door was shut. [11] "Later, the other bridesmaids also came. 'Sir! Sir!' they said. 'Open the door for us!' [12] "But he replied, 'What I'm about to tell you is true. I don't know you.' [13] "So keep watch. You do not know the day or the hour that the groom will come.

The Wisdom of Honesty

We all know honesty is the key to any relationship. To show dishonesty in business dealings is not only immoral but illegal. Aside from the moral and legal issues it is simply bad for business. Every business has its reputation following it whether good or bad. When clients hear of dishonesty you can bet they will not be clients for long. Of course we know this, but the more likely danger for my readers is the possibility that you might lie to yourself. When times are good we take credit, but when bad we might try and assign blame. If you take credit or assign blame without carefully considering the true cause of each you might well be lying to yourself and destroying company morale. Be sure that you are truthful when it comes to your own capabilities. If you down play your strengths you will miss opportunities. If you fail to recognize you weakness you risk having them derail a success in the making. In short be honest in your dealings with others, but perhaps even more important be honest with yourself.

From Man:

"Honesty is the cornerstone of all success, without which confidence and ability to perform shall cease to exist."

--Mary Kay Ash

"The highest compact we can make with our fellow is, - 'Let there be truth between us two forever more.'"

--Ralph Waldo Emerson

From God:

Exodus 18:21

[21] "But choose men of ability from all of the people. They must have respect for God. You must be able to trust them. They must not try to get money by cheating others. Appoint them as officials over thousands, hundreds, fifties and tens.

Deuteronomy 16:19-20

[19] Do what is right. Treat everyone the same. Don't take money from people who want special favors. It makes those who are wise close their eyes to the truth. It twists the words of those who do what is right. [20] Follow only what is right. If you do, you will live. You will take over the land the Lord your God is giving you.

2 Samuel 22:21

[21] "The Lord has been good to me because I do what is right. He has rewarded me because I lead a pure life.

The Wisdom of Teams

Teams are part of almost all organizations. Owners are parts of regional teams and employees are part of everything from process to cross functional teams. The great thing about teams is they are varied people with a wide array of experience, talent, and drive. The problem with teams is the politics and egos. When choosing a team make sure you have an extremely well defined goal, make sure everyone knows what they are trying to do. Insure a leader is appointed. It is better if you appoint them. A leader needs to be chosen for their ability to complete the task, not by popularity. Then you must delegate the authority along with the task. A team that must report every detail can get nothing done. Once you have chosen a great team, selected a solid leader and given them the authority and instruction remove the last obstacle…YOU. You should receive reports weekly or as often as needed to keep you informed, but unless the task looks as if it will not be complete stay out of their way. If you have chosen wisely have the confidence that they will succeed.

From Man:

The best executive is the one who has sense enough to pick good men to do what he wants done, and self-restraint enough to keep from meddling with them while they do it. -Theodore Roosevelt

Appreciate everything your associates do for the business. Nothing else can quite substitute for a few well-chosen, well-timed, sincere words of praise. They're absolutely free and worth a fortune. - Sam Walton founder of Wal-Mart

From God:

Nehemiah 2:17-18 (MSG)

Then I gave them my report: "Face it: we're in a bad way here. Jerusalem is a wreck; its gates are burned up. Come—let's build the wall of Jerusalem and not live with this disgrace any longer." I told them how God was supporting me and how the king was backing me up. They said, "We're with you. Let's get started." They rolled up their sleeves, ready for the good work.

You can find more
Wisdom for Business from God and man
at www.TheNewRuleofThree.com

Now on to the Experience!

Table of Contents

Introduction

You might be asking, "Why should I buy your book?" If your business has slow growth, if your business is not what you dreamed it would be, or if you just want to take your business to the next level, this book is for you.

So who am I? I am an author, speaker, marketing consultant, and certified strategic business coach. I am the founder and chief executive officer of Marketing and Business Dynamics. I have been on syndicated radio and cable and broadcast television, and I have been published in the *Houston Business Journal, The Daily Court Review, Houston's Daily Business Newspaper* as "The One Minute Marketer," with daily marketing tips and a weekly business column. I have three columns in Go Local Magazine and am a Small Business Examiner, on Examiner.com

My awards and recognition began when I received the Rookie of the Year Award, for achieving exceptional sales increases, from a national restaurant chain. It continued throughout my career when I received a chairman's award for leading a group of sales professionals as they educated themselves on presentation skills, speaking techniques, and appointment setting. The combination of education, role-play, and practice created a highly successful lead exchange network that generated numerous leads for each other. I was named Start Ups Nation's "Spotlight on Success" in September 2005. Most recently, my work led to being recognized as a B.E.S.T. Business and receiving the 2006 Business Partner of the Year Award for developing a relationship between a local school district and a quick service restaurant. The award was presented by the Cypress-Fairbanks Independent School District and the State of Texas. Your business should be a great success. You should reach the goals you dreamed of when you started your business. In this book, I will give you the tools to create an experience for your clients that will not only have them coming back, but also telling their friends and families that they would be crazy not to do business with you.

That is the power of The Experience!

The books *One Minute Manager* and *Who Moved My Cheese?* are excellent examples of using a narrative to convey a message. Far be it from me not to borrow from the authors of these great books. The great thing about stories is that we see our own life experiences in them. In this book, you may discover an experience that would fit well with your business.

This book will begin with the journey of "Bob," a business owner whose business has been confronted with stagnant growth and painfully average customer service. While Bob is not a real person and some of the situations are based in fiction, the vast majority is drawn from observations and real events from my personal and professional life. We will examine the themes played out in Bob's journey and challenge you to take your own voyage into the realms of "The Experience." One of my all-time favorite comedians is Bill Cosby. In a classic routine from *Bill Cosby: Himself,* he says, "Let me tell you a story ..." before he shares a bit of wisdom disguised as comedy. Motivational guru Zig Ziglar has taught us that a story is the best way to teach.

So, with that, Bob's story begins ...

Chapter 1
Welcome to Shinobi

As Bob walked past a maze of small, gray cubicles to his office, he thought of the presentation and tour he had given last week. He was eagerly awaiting a visit from his friend John. John was on the team for Highend Systems, the company Bob had presented to last week. The planning and presentation represented a huge investment of time and resources, but the account would be the largest Bob's company had ever received.

The preliminary meetings had been excellent, so much so that John confided in Bob that the account would be awarded to either Bob's or one other company. The final presentation and tour would seal the deal.

Bob glanced up from his desk as his secretary opened the door and ushered John in. "Good morning," Bob said enthusiastically. Bob's face fell somewhat at the pause before John's response. "Good to see you again Bob, I just wish I had better news," John said quietly. "I am afraid the team has chosen to award the account to the other firm," he added.

Disappointed, Bob looked away. He collected himself and turned back to his friend. "May I ask what tipped the scales?" Bob requested. "Was it the price point, or something in my final presentation?"

"No," answered John, "in fact your price was a bit lower, and your final
presentation was up to your normal excellent standards. It was the tour that clinched the choice. Bob, I tried to point out positives about your company, but they were simply matched by your competition."

Taken aback Bob asked, "What was wrong with the tour? I conducted it personally; everything was as it should be." "I know what you mean,"
said John, "everything was fine, just fine. When we took the tour of your
competition," John paused, "something was just different, it seemed to pop, it's hard to explain. There was just an energy there that convinced the team to go with them, even though they were a little more expensive."

"I really thought it would turn out differently. I know you have the technical ability and a better price, I am sorry it didn't work out Bob. I will keep your company in mind for the next contract," John assured him.

Bob decided then and there that he would walk through the entire tour again looking for the slightest thing that might have gone wrong. He marched to the lobby and watched as his receptionist, from behind her desk, paused from a phone call to briefly greet an arriving client, and motioned for him to take a seat in the lobby.

The lobby was well-lit and furnished nicely. Bob noticed the magazines were out of date and plied up a bit, but nothing that would have cost him the account. As he continued down the hallway, into what he called the pen, a few heads raised above the gray cubicles in a Dilbert-style greeting of "Hello Mr. Brown". All his employees were dressed according to the company's professional dress code and the cubicles were free of clutter aside from a few family pictures.

Everything was well within the professional norms. Bob moved through the hallways to the production area. He called to the foreman and asked how everything was going. The foreman assured Bob that the shipment would be ready on schedule and turned to leave. Bob pressed the question and the foreman defensively continued that his production facility was well within the guidelines set by Bob, the Union, and OSHA. He reminded Bob that

he had not had a late shipment in the two years he had been in charge. Bob said, "So everything is fine here." "Yes," answered the foreman, "everything is fine!"
As Bob turned and walked away he heard the foreman mutter, "The suits never come in here without wanting something rushed or to bust our chops."

Bob continued to tour his own business and concluded that everything was fine - just fine. Bob decided at that moment that he would make some changes in his customer service, both for internal and external customers.

One year later…
Disappointed, Bob tossed the results of the customer service survey back into his briefcase. The changes he had implemented had not generated the results he wanted. Bob's customers were not dissatisfied with the service his business provided, yet it had not been rated excellent, either. Sales were stagnant. There had been no improvement the previous quarter or the quarter before that. It seemed that Bob's business was average and would remain that way despite his attempts to change it.

As the plane made its descent, Bob's thoughts turned to the reasons he had just flown to Houston. He had heard that Mr. Kalibar of Shinobi Enterprises had some new and interesting ideas on customer service, real cutting-edge stuff, and Bob's company could really use some sprucing up in that area. Bob had called Kalibar and asked if he would share his thoughts.

"I would be delighted to," Kalibar said. Bob waited for Kalibar to expand, but he didn't. Finally, Bob asked Kalibar what his ideas were. "Oh, I'm sorry," Kalibar said. "I can't possibly tell you about it. You'll have to fly here and experience it. I have time next week if you'd like to spend a few days with us."

Bob, slightly irritated that Kalibar would not simply explain himself over the phone, quipped, "Are you sure you want me to witness all your secrets?"

"Certainly," Kalibar returned cheerfully. "It's your business. It would be different if you followed my every step—but you won't follow my every step, nor should you. Please speak with my assistant, Jessica, and let her know when you will be arriving."

Just like that, Bob was transferred, and a cheery female voice said, "This is Jessica. How can I be seriously helpful today?"

Bob was amazed to hear himself setting up a meeting for the following Tuesday. "Great," Jessica said. "I look forward to meeting you." And that was that.

Bob came back to the present as the pilot announced in a monotone that the plane was beginning its descent and asked the passengers to return to their seats and fasten their seat belts. After Bob exited the plane, he followed his typical business trip routine, collecting his bags and making his way to the taxi stand.

The cab driver followed Bob's directions to a stand-alone, two-story building that could have been a home, club, or office—not at all what Bob had been expecting. He double-checked the address and found this to be the place. Bob tipped the cabbie and proceeded inside, his bags in tow.

The offices of Shinobi Enterprises weren't anything like Bob had expected. The decor was a mix of Japanese and modern American styles complete with low tables and decorative paper screens. A simple, functional black desk with a computer, fax, and phone on top and inviting futons lined the walls of half of the office.

The receptionist's desk was against the wall across from the futons, but it was the wall facing the door that caught Bob's eye. A vintage Space Invaders game sat against that wall. Bob couldn't believe a respected marketing guru would keep such a frivolous item in his office.
Before Bob could think of reasons to house such an out-of-place object in the waiting room he was intercepted by a smiling woman with an outstretched hand. Instinctively, he shook it.

"You must be Bob! Welcome to Shinobi Enterprises. My name is Jessica. Just leave your bags right here. We'll look after them while you meet with Mr. Kalibar. You're a few minutes early."
Motioning to the black desk, she added, "Please feel free to have a look, and if you need to check your e-mail or fax something to your office, please use any of our resources."

"One more thing," she grinned. "No quarters needed."

Bob glanced over at the arcade game, and when he turned back to ask why it was in the lobby, Jessica was gone.

It was such an odd thing to have in a professional setting. Bob had to walk over and look at it. The machine seemed to be in good condition, with some minor blemishes on the controls and scratches on the screen. Sure enough, it had credits, but Bob did not play.
"Mr. Kalibar will see you now," Jessica said with a smile. "Have an outrageously informative meeting."

Notes

Chapter 2
The First Sighting

Bob thought the lobby was strange, but Kalibar's office reached a whole new level of oddness. The Japanese-influenced decor continued. There were no video games, but a menagerie of action figures, Superman, Batman, Luke Skywalker, and others were lined up in small formations on one wall. Fine Japanese watercolors decorated the other. A large, arched window on the wall opposite the door flooded the room with natural light.

Amid this eclectic decor sat a plain-looking man at a simple, dark wood desk in front of the window. Kalibar appeared to be in his late thirties. He was slightly balding and offered an infectious grin. Bob was slightly dumbfounded. The video game had struck him as peculiar, but the combination of the toys and the art was just a little too much for him to take in all at once. His wonder apparently showed on his face.

Kalibar chuckled and offered him a seat. "You are wondering about the video game and my collection, I take it."

"It's different," Bob offered, trying to be polite.

"Really? It strikes most people as a bit odd," Kalibar said with a smile. Shifting uncomfortably in his seat, Bob replied, "Well, I—"

"Most people see it that way at first," Kalibar interrupted. "We are in the business of crafting experiences and outrageously good marketing for folks. You can't do that if you take yourself too seriously. I always let prospective employees spend a few minutes waiting. If they play a game or two, I give them a mark in their favor. We don't need any uptight, overly serious types around here."

Notes

Chapter 3
Flying the Average Skies

"But enough about us. How was your flight?" Kalibar asked.
"Fine," answered Bob, anxious to get past the pleasantries and into the meat of the discussion.

"I would like you to share some of the details of your flight with me," Kalibar pressed. "Did it leave on time?"

This is just plain crazy, Bob thought. I flew all this way, and he wants to talk about a mundane plane trip. My business isn't growing like I want it to and he's waste time talking about my flight?
"Well," Bob said, "It left about ten minutes after the scheduled time, but that's about average."

"Go on," said Kalibar. "Tell me about the flight attendants."

"They were OK, I guess."

"How so?"

"They brought me peanuts, or maybe pretzels, and then drinks came around. That was about it."

"Really?" Kalibar said. "You know, I think Brad in billing recently returned from his vacation. If you ask Jessica, I am sure she will direct you to his office." With that, Kalibar stood to walk Bob to the door. "After you talk to Brad, grab some lunch. We'll meet back here at 2:00 pm, OK?"

"Excuse me, Mr. Kalibar. I flew here to talk to you," Bob said as politely as he could.

"And you will. After lunch. 2:00 pm," Kalibar said, tapping his index finger on the face of his watch. Before Bob could protest further, he was in the hallway looking at Kalibar's closed door.
Jessica appeared instantly. "May I help you find something or someone?" she asked knowingly.
"Yes," Bob answered, bewildered. "I'm supposed to speak with Brad in billing."

"Sure. Right this way," Jessica said just before marching down the hall.

Bob stood for a moment and considered his options. Part of him wanted to leave this crazy place, but after a second, he reconsidered. Maybe there was something he could learn from Kalibar that would make the trip worthwhile.

The wide hallway Bob walked down was the most normal part of the building he'd seen so far: dark gray carpet, standard overhead lighting, and neutral-colored walls with motivational placards. Bob stopped, curious about a large room to his right.

"What is—"
"It's our corporate gym and dojo area. Mr. Kalibar believes that if you're in shape physically, you'll be happier and more productive at work and at home."

The spacious room was stocked with exercise bikes, treadmills, and elliptical trainers. Part of the room was filled with mats, a kicking bag, and what looked like a plastic mannequin.

Bob stared and asked, "Mr. Kalibar paid for all of this?"
"Of course. We also have a strict 'no work on Sundays and only on Saturday if it's an emergency' rule," Jessica said. "Some of us go to church, some just spend time with families, and some watch the Texans play. That keeps us spiritually fit.

"Of course, we are all encouraged to be lifelong learners. Mr. Kalibar sends us to seminars and workshops. I recently attended a Zig Ziglar two-day motivational program. I'm still pumped up," she said before changing the subject. "Brad's office is at the end of the hall."

Bob was somewhat relieved to see no video games or toys, just a regular office with pictures of family and a computer atop a normal desk.
"Brad, this is Bob. He came to learn about our idea of customer service.

Do you have a few minutes?"
"Sure," answered Brad. "Come in and have a seat."
"How can I be amazingly helpful today?" Brad asked.

"Mr. Kalibar mentioned you recently flew in from a vacation. He told me to ask about your flight," Bob began hesitantly.

"Sure," Brad answered enthusiastically. "I flew on Southwest. I always fly Southwest when I can. Did you know they take off on time like 95 percent of the time?"

"No," Bob said, surprised.

"When you have an eight-year-old and a sixteen-month-old, that's very important. And their staff is really great. We got to the gate a little early, and the gate attendant gave my little boy a set of pilot wings and told him where to stand so he could see the planes take off and land. When it was time to board, they let us board first. One of the gate attendants even helped my wife with the diaper bag."

"Really?" Bob said.

"Yeah," Brad continued. "The flight attendants were even better, dancing and singing through the safety information, tossing pretzels down the aisle, handing them to a couple of people that didn't want to try and catch them.

I guess I looked like a big eater, because they gave me two bags. They served drinks shortly after takeoff and were quick with refills when we needed them.

Those flight attendants really made the trip go by fast, a rarity with two kids."

"Sounds like your trip was better than mine. I'm glad to hear the fight attendants were doing their jobs."

"Oh, it wasn't just the attendants, Bob. The pilots were fantastic, too. They kept us informed with light banter. The captain even pointed out a flock of invisible flying pigs to the kids. I was a little surprised to see a few adults looking out the window as well," Brad chuckled.

"Really? The pilots did all of that?" Bob was amazed.

"Yep. And the attendant helped my wife and me with our bags when we landed. It was a fantastic experience," Brad said, smiling. "Is there anything else I can help you with
?"

"No, thanks," Bob said, feeling his stomach rumble. "I think I'll get some lunch."

Notes

Chapter 4
Lunch

Bob sat in Kalibar's office fidgeting with the mint wrapper from the restaurant where he'd had lunch. This trip was not going as he had expected.

He had expected a conference room and some sort of presentation, maybe talking points on a handout to be discussed over lunch. He hadn't expected Brad's story of his fantastic airline experience. Surely Kalibar did not expect Bob's staff to sing and dance like the flight attendants for Southwest Airlines! That would be absurd. They were professionals.

Kalibar strolled into the room with a smile and sat down at his desk. "So,
Bob, how was lunch?"
"Fine."
"Really? Just 'fine?'"

Seeing Kalibar's slight smile, Bob decided to elaborate. "I waited a few minutes for my table, I was seated by an attentive hostess who took my drink order, the waiter was there promptly, and the food was out in ten minutes, as I had ordered it."

"So, it was fine?"

Bob sat for a moment, contemplating what kind of game Kalibar might be playing. Obviously, he was looking for something better than "fine," but Bob's patience had run out. Wanting Kalibar to get to the point, Bob said, "Yes, it was fine."

Kalibar pushed a button on his intercom. "Nicole?"

"Yes, Mr. Kalibar?"

"Where did you have lunch today?"
"The Potato Patch, sir."
"Great. Do you have a minute to speak with my friend, Bob?" Kalibar asked. "Sure," Nicole answered.
"You should talk to Nicole about *her* lunch," Kalibar said, walking to the door. This time, Bob didn't move.

"Listen, Kalibar, I agreed to fly all this way to meet you because I thought you had some new ideas to grow my business. I didn't take time out of my busy schedule to waste time talking to Brad or Nicole or Tom or Dick or Jane or anyone else. I came here for some solutions, and I want them now." Bob's impatience was clear.

Slowly, Kalibar closed his office door, turned, walked back to the desk and sat on the edge. He smiled.

"I understand your frustration. If you remember, I told you on the phone I couldn't tell you about what I had to offer your business. You would have to experience it. Trust me, Bob. I'm not wasting your time. I could explain that *the Experience* is about increasing the value of what you offer; that to create an experience you would have to develop a theme. I could mention that engaging the senses is important and that you must choose between being real, fake fake, or a real fake. I could even spend an hour explaining the four realms of the Experience. I could tell you how creating an experience can make you an army of unpaid sales people.

As I said, however, you must experience *the Experience* to make sense of it. To fully grasp what I am teaching you, I need you to have the context of this journey.

"If you will bear with me for the rest of your stay, you will begin to understand what I'm trying to show you."

Bob let out a long sigh. "Fine. What do I need to do?"

"Simple. Speak to Nicole about her lunch," Kalibar said, still smiling.

Once again, Bob found himself being herded down the spacious hallway by Jessica. "Nicole is fairly new here," Jessica explained. "She has been making killer waves in marketing ever since she arrived last year."

Bob entered, to his relief, another fairly regular office. Rattan furnishings and pictures of beaches and surf gave it a hint of Hawaiian style. A tan, athletic young lady with a ready smile stepped from behind the small desk and greeted Bob.

"I'm Nicole. How can I make your day sunnier?"

"Mr. Kalibar said I should ask you about your lunch," Bob said, somewhat surprised to hear the words come out of his mouth.

"Sure," Nicole said. "It's Tuesday. I always go to the Potato Patch on Tuesday. Mr. Kalibar lets us choose our own lunch hour to accommodate our and our clients' schedules. I generally go a little early. But, when I got there today, it was already pretty busy. So, I put my name on the list, sat down, and was ready to duck."

"Ready to duck?" asked Bob.

"Oh, yes," Nicole said, grinning. "The Potato Patch is known for its great down-home cooking, particularly its homemade rolls. But that's not all. While you're waiting, or even during your meal, if you want a roll, you just shout out or motion to one of the …," She thought a moment before continuing, "roll guys, and they send the rolls flying your way.

"I used to play beach volleyball in California. I'm telling you, these guys can throw. By the time I'd finished my roll and ducked a few less accurate throws, the friend I was meeting had arrived, and our table was ready.

He's a Patch veteran, too, so he knew what to expect. Real home cooking takes a little longer than some restaurants, you know. So when the waiter asks you what you'd like to drink, I always recommend the sweet tea. They serve it in a huge glass so you don't run out.

"Now, they do have appetizers on the menu, but I don't know why. I certainly never saw anything like this back in California, but at the Patch, they bring around bins of fried okra and fried green tomatoes. For the brave, they have some kind of jalapeno thing. I don't really have the palate for that.

I'm not a native Texan, after all," she said with a grin.
"I'm always half full when the main dish arrives. I generally get the lunch portion chicken fried steak. It almost completely covers the plate. It's a good thing I like white gravy on my mashed potatoes; otherwise I'd need another plate.

The food is always hot and fresh, and it costs me an extra hour in the gym, but it's worth it. The whole place just has that feeling of home, even for a Californian in Texas."

Bob thanked her for her insight and made his way back to the lobby, where he briefly considered playing a game of Space Invaders.

Instead, he reflected on what Nicole had told him.

Mr. Kalibar appeared through the entrance. "How did your chat with Nicole go?" he inquired.

"I don't see how all these anecdotes about airline travel and restaurants help me with my business."

"Fair enough," said Kalibar. "I'll tell you what. Speak with Lyssa. She's my right hand around here. Ask her to make a reservation for a dinner, my treat. Trust me. She knows all the best of fine dining places around here. We will talk about it tomorrow morning at ten. Okay, great. See you tomorrow."

And with that, Mr. Kalibar disappeared into his office.

Bob certainly was not going to turn down a free dinner. If nothing else, a nice meal would be the one benefit of the trip. With directions from Jessica,

Bob found himself in front of a waved-glass door that read, "If you're having a great day, come in any time. If you're having a rough day, get in here now!"

Bob knocked lightly, and a smooth feminine voice from behind the door answered, "Please come in." Bob entered a room filled with black furniture, fine silver inlay, and a desk with an equally stylish young lady sitting behind it.

"You must be Bob," Lyssa greeted him. "I hope Mr. Kalibar doesn't have you running around in circles too much."

Bob smiled, still evaluating the worth of his trip. "It certainly has been interesting," he quipped.

"Yes," answered Lyssa, "Mr. Kalibar sure is interesting, if nothing else.

Now tell me, do you like French or Italian?"

Bob decided that a fine French restaurant would be free of flying snails or other hazardous activities and chose accordingly. "Great choice," Lyssa said.

"I know Fredrick at Chez Pierre. I am sure he can get you a table if you don't mind an early dinner."

Bob agreed and listened as Lyssa spoke easily with the maitre d' and made the arrangements. "May I ask you a question?" Bob asked.

"Certainly," Lyssa answered.

"I noticed everyone goes by his or her first name with the exception of Mr. Kalibar," Bob said. "He mentioned you were his right hand around here.
Don't you ever call him by his first name?"
"Actually, I don't," Lyssa said thoughtfully. "I haven't really thought about it. He treats everyone the same, from me to the mail clerk. If you ask me why we use his last name, I would say it's because he's the boss."

"Ah, 'the boss,'" said Bob, nodding his head knowingly.

"I don't think you quite understand what I mean," Lyssa said. "It's not a way of getting respect. He earns that from the way he treats us.

 Someone has to be the boss because, ultimately, he has to be held responsible for what goes on and make sure things keep moving in the right direction. It seems to me that someone of that nature should be a Mr. or Mrs. Somebody. I think we're lucky that our leader is Mr. Kalibar.

"You're all set for five pm. Fredrick will send the bill my way tomorrow. Enjoy your dinner."

Notes

Chapter 5
Dinner at Chez Pierre

Following the directions that Lyssa gave him, Bob found his way to Chez Pierre slightly after five. He asked for Fredrick, and a young man in a tuxedo greeted him. Before Bob could introduce himself, the young man said, "Ah, you must be Lyssa's friend!"

"Yes," Bob replied.

"Welcome to Chez Pierre. Would you like a quiet table, to be in the middle of things, or a seat at the bar where you can enjoy a fine smoke with your dinner?"

"I think a quiet table with a view of the action would be nice."
"Certainly, sir. And would you like to start with a glass of wine this evening? I will have your server bring it as soon as your table is ready."

"Yes, thank you."

Bob was impressed with the red-carpet treatment. Certainly Lyssa was well connected. However, when the next guest arrived, Bob saw that he also was greeted by name and received the same treatment and service.

Bob realized that Chez Pierre rolled out the red carpet for everyone. When

Fredrick showed him to his table, a glass of red wine was waiting for him.

"Jonous will be your server this evening. He is fluent in French and
English and is very knowledgeable about our menu. Should you need
anything, please let me know."

As Bob looked over the menu, he heard light, airy but unfamiliar music
in the background. He noticed a woman playing a grand harp in the center of
the dining room. The music was quite beautiful, as was the decor, the place
setting, and most everything else he saw.

 Jonous stood by silently until Bob came out of his musings. After a few
questions about the menu for Jonous, Bob decided on the roast duck with
mango salsa and escargot as an appetizer.

When Bob finished the escargot, he was a little surprised to
see Jonous headed his way with a cup of orange sherbet. Upon reaching the
table, Jonous noted the slight confusion on Bob's face and quickly explained
that in some parts of France, sherbet is used to cleanse the palate so the
flavor of the main course can be fully enjoyed. As Bob finished his meal, he
noticed the dining room was nearly full. He recalled that he had been a last-
minute
reservation. Despite that, the service and the meal had been excellent.

Jonous arrived with a dessert tray. Despite the temptation, Bob declined.
Jonous thanked him for coming and said, "Your dinner is taken care of.

Please stay and enjoy the music as long as you wish. I will be by should you
need anything further. Just let me know."

Bob was pleasantly surprised at this, since he was expecting to be politely
hurried along due to the booming business. He left Jonous a 25 percent tip.

After dinner, Bob reflected on the service he had received. He carefully
considered what had happened and was up early the next morning, hopeful
about his meeting with Kalibar.

True to Bob's expectation, Kalibar bid him a good morning and followed it
with, "How was your dinner last night?"

Bob answered, "I may be getting the hang of this. Let me tell you what I saw last night." Kalibar smiled, "Go right ahead."

"First," Bob began, "Lyssa was able to get me a reservation on short notice.

Even though I was running a little late, the restaurant did not give away my table. The host called me and some other guest by name, something that always makes me feel special. The whole place was elegantly decorated, and they had a wonderful harpist playing, even before their busy time.

"At one point, my waiter brought out sherbet. I didn't know why, but he managed to explain it to me without being condescending. And, now that I think about it, they asked for a smoking preference in a way that would allow them to keep the smokers in one area and the non-smokers in another without seeming judgmental.

"Even when the restaurant was getting busy and I had finished my meal, my server invited me to stay as long as I liked." Bob concluded, "I think I am really getting the concept of how this experience thing works in a service and hospitality industry, but I'm still not sure how it will translate into a professional setting."

"It's funny that you should mention that," Kalibar said. "I know just who you should talk to about that. Here is the address. It's just a few blocks from here. Ask for Jim. He is the owner of the game and hobby store where I buy my comics."

Notes

Chapter 6
The Comic Book Store

Bob couldn't remember the last time he had been in a comic book store. As he pushed open the glass doors and walked into Intergalactic Comics and Games, he tried to imagine what the owner of such an establishment could possibly teach him that would help his own business.

At first glance, the shop was much as Bob expected—games, comics, and figures neatly lining the shelves; posters of heroes and villains adorning the walls. Upon closer inspection, however, Bob noticed that only one of any given item was on display. Even the comic books were individually shelved.

The relative quiet surprised him as well. After all, school was out for the summer; he'd imagined on his way over that the place would be full of kids playing those popular trading card games.

As Bob surveyed the shop with a mix of curiosity and skepticism, a young clerk dressed in a pressed polo shirt and dress slacks approached and very politely said, "Welcome to Intergalactic. My name is Dennis. May I help you find something?"

Bob was a little taken aback by the clerk's level of professionalism. Truth be told, he had expected to be only half-acknowledged by a kid in a Batman T-shirt and jeans.

"I was hoping to speak with Jim," Bob said.

"Sure. I'll get him for you. Have a look around," Dennis said as he headed behind the glass display cases.

"Hello, Sir," said Jim. "Welcome to my shop. How can I help you?"

"You can call me Bob. Mr. Kalibar sent me over to hear what you have to say about the customer service experience," Bob said.

"Nice to meet you Bob, Mr. Kalibar is one of my oldest and dearest customers," Jim said with a grin. "So, what do you think of my store?"

"I noticed a few things that seem a little … well, odd for a comic book store," Bob continued.

"How so?" Jim asked.

"Well, first off, I have never been met at the door by a greeter or whatever he was."

"Oh, Dennis. He is my best afternoon salesman," Jim said just loudly enough for his voice to carry across the room. Dennis grinned at the compliment and continued helping a young boy find a card he wanted.

"I also noticed that you only have one of everything. What do you do when someone buys something? Most comic stores have a ton of stock on the shelves."

"So you frequent comic and card shops back home?" asked Jim.

"Well, no, not really," admitted Bob. "I don't think I have been in one since I was a kid. Are they all like this now?"

"I certainly hope not. Otherwise, I wouldn't be anything special," said Jim. "No, we are the only one of this kind that I know of. You see, I based the store off my old job," answered Jim.

"What was that?" Bob asked.

"I don't mean to brag, but I was the number one salesperson in Texas for Lexus," replied Jim.

Bob looked around. "I hope you won't take offense, but what does luxury car sales have to do with this?"

"Pretty much everything is the same, except here, I see people every week, not every three years. That makes it much easier to build a relationship with them," answered Jim.

Bob looked around again, failing to see the similarities in a $50,000 car and a $3 comic book.

"I know what you're thinking," Jim said. "But think about when you walk into a fine dealership. Aren't you greeted by a host or hostess of sorts?"

"Well, yes," Bob admitted.

"As far as there being one of every item on display, well, you certainly don't have every color and equipment package on the floor, do you? Employing that practice here ensures that everyone who comes in gets personal attention from our staff. They simply tell Dennis what they are looking for, and he gets it from the inventory.

This interaction makes customers feel special, and it also allows Dennis to get a feel for their tastes. That way, he can tell them about other titles or games that might be of interest to them."

"And give you a chance to sell more, right?" asked Bob.

"We certainly like to run a profitable business, and we do make suggestions to our clients," admitted Jim. "I don't ever try to sell anyone anything."

"What do you mean isn't suggestion and selling the same thing?" Bob asked.

"One of the biggest things I learned in the automobile industry was that people hate to be sold to. Give them the information they need to make an informed decision, and you will likely make the sale. Even if you don't, you have shown that you have the customers' best interest at heart. That leads to referrals and repeat customers."

"Hmm, interesting. So what else do you do around here?" inquired Bob.

"Let's take a look in back, shall we?" said Jim.
As they moved towards the door leading behind the display cases, Bob noticed two doors off to the right. As he neared them, he heard somewhat of a commotion. Jim seemed not to notice, until Bob stopped to peer into one of the windows.

"You might have been wondering where the kids are," Jim remarked. "These are my game rooms. I provide them free to the kids after school and all summer for general play. On weekends they house a tournament of one type or another from open to close. There are soda and vending machines, and I have a few video games in room two.
"These rooms," Jim continued, "allow me to have all the fun and ruckus that kids love about a game store and still maintain the leisurely, organized atmosphere that you noticed when you came in."
"I would have thought kids made up most of your customers," Bob said.

"Actually, more than half our comic subscribers are over twenty-one," Jim clarified.

"Subscribers?"

"Sure," answered Jim. "When I was in the automobile industry, I saw people about every two or three years. Even though our relationship was limited, I still kept records of birth dates and anniversaries, so that I could send cards and such. I apply a similar concept here.

"As I mentioned before, I see most of our customers once a week. They have a box, here along this wall, each with a list like this."
Bob noticed a three-by-five-inch index card with title types on the top corner of each box.

"We fill their list of titles and add any crossover or special comics featuring their favorite characters," said Jim. "They are not required to buy the extras, of course, but because of the relationship we've established, we can usually tell when they will want something. I'd say about 75 percent buy our suggestions. They get a little more enjoyment, and we get another sale. So you see, it's truly a win-win arrangement.

"I help their wives pick out graphic novels or a certain action figure for birthdays and Christmas. I have a few of their children hooked on comics as well."

A young woman raised her head from a computer screen as the two approached.

"Bob, I'd like you to meet Lisa. She's my best Web salesperson." Lisa grinned as she stood to shake Bob's hand.

"It's nice to meet you, Lisa. Please, tell me more about what you do here."

"Well, I guess I try to carry our strong commitment to personalized service and the same feeling you get in the store to the Web site. This is important, as 30 percent of our clients are Web-based, including many military folks overseas that can't just run out and buy a copy of their favorite titles."

"I know I should learn there is always an answer," Bob said, "but how can you translate what is here in the real world to online?"

"First I had to see what people like about us," answered Lisa. "Many online comic book sites open with a tremendous amount of Flash effects and lengthy intros. It turns out most people skip them after the first visit.

"Those sites have forgotten that most people who use the Web for purchases are looking to save time, not be impressed with effects. So just like our brick-and-mortar store, you can find virtually any category with one click from the front page.

"We do offer online chat and even some online gaming for those who play on the Web," Lisa continued, "but from the home page, you can bypass all that and get straight to what you want. The orders are e-mailed to me, and I reply with any add-ons or specials I think they might like, if they signed up for that service. From there, the orders go to Glen in shipping."

"Lisa also puts rare items on eBay from time to time, more to attract new online clients than for profit. But as I said before, I am a big fan of profit." Jim laughed, then continued, "You will like Glen. He is my best bag-and-boarder."

"Now wait," Bob grunted. "I've noticed that you refer to each staff member as 'the best' this or that. Why is that? Are they the only ones that do the job?"

"In some cases, yes, replied Jim, "but I mean it every time I say it. Glen, for instance, is not what I would call a people person. He is soft-spoken and a little reserved, and he would never make a suggestion if his life depended on it.

He is, however, great at handling the books with great care and speed, not only in putting the books and backboards in the bags, but also in prepping them for mailing as well. He is a whiz with the label machine and postage meter."

"So he is more limited than your other employees," stated Bob.

"Far from it," Jim replied with a chuckle. "Dennis would lose his mind in less than a week back here, as would I. When 30 percent of your clients' products go through one man's hands, that person had better be good.

"I make it a point to hire only the best and I have found that everyone is the best at something so I hire them for what they are best at."

True to expectation, Glen spoke quietly about what he did and mentioned that he always used first-class or priority mail to make sure the books arrived in good condition and on time. During the holidays, he called on FedEx to meet the rush of last-minute shoppers.

With that, he simply returned to his work with a steady flow and organized eye that made him valuable to the store.

"Well, Bob, I hope that gives you an idea of how we do things around here. If you are still in town on Saturday, come by. We cut a deal with a local photographer; for the price of five cans of food, to be donated to the Houston Food Bank, you too can have your picture taken with Batman," Jim said in good-natured jest.

"The event always attracts people to the shop. Last year we picked up two press releases from it. The photographer donates pictures that have his name and number on the back. We all get the goodwill of doing something for others, and of course, the food bank gets the food. It's another of those win-win deals."

Bob thanked Jim for his hospitality and headed for the door. "Just a second, Bob," Jim called. "Are you headed back to Mr. Kalibar's office?"

Bob nodded.

"Would you mind taking these to him? It's this week's shipment of books.

You see, I have many of my subscribers' credit cards on file so they can grab and go if they don't have time to stay and talk."

Bob took the books willingly, no longer surprised that a professional, at least in Kalibar's case, would read comics.

Notes

Chapter 7
Back to the Office

Bob walked into the now familiar lobby carrying a bag of comic books. As he greeted Jessica, he realized that the Space Invaders game no longer seemed so out of place to him.

Jessica phoned Kalibar and instructed Bob to go right in.

"Jim asked me to bring these to you," Bob said as he handed over the comics.

"Ah, yes, thank you," Kalibar answered. "I wonder what extras he found for me this week. Did you find anything Jim had to say useful?"

"I believe so," Bob said. "He seems to spend as much effort creating an experience for his employees as he does for his customers."

"I think you may be right about that," Kalibar agreed.

"It makes perfect sense for him," said Bob, "as almost all of his employees have direct contact with his customers. If he can create the Experience with them, it will automatically carry over to the clients."

"I have shared with you some of the locals' ideas of creating an experience," Kalibar said, "but I would be remiss if I did not mention the grandfather of experience. That, of course, would be Disney."

Notes

Chapter 8
The Magic Kingdom

"Tell me about your last vacation, if you would, Bob."

"Well," Bob said, "it was last summer. We headed to the coast for some fun on the beach and shopping for the wife. I am pretty sure I should have taken Southwest Airlines, based on what Brad told me yesterday. So I will skip forward to our hotel.

"It was a nice three-star hotel. Upon our arrival, a bellboy met us at the curb to help with the luggage. We went to the desk and checked in. They had our reservation, so everything went smoothly.

The bellboy helped us up to our room without saying much. The room was a nice size, as we expected, with two double beds—one for the wife and me, and one for Bob Jr. Overall, it was fine." Bob smiled.

"I too took a vacation last year, in September as I recall," Kalibar said. "We traveled to Florida. Disney World, to be precise. After we landed, we collected our bags and followed the plentiful signs to the shuttle area, where a hotel shuttle was waiting to carry us to the Polynesian Resort, one of Disney's on-site hotels. The shuttle was testimony to the rich theme soon to come: it was completely painted to resemble a tropical beach scene sporting Mickey and Minnie Mouse in full beach regalia.

"The driver helped put the bags in back, and we found ourselves whisked away toward our lodging. When we arrived, we were greeted by two young people wearing Hawaiian shirts. As the young lady of the pair escorted us to the check-in counter, she explained that, as guests of this hotel, we had an hour's extra admission to any of the parks. She also informed us of our choices of monorail, steamboat, or shuttle van to and from the parks. After asking if we had any questions, she smiled and returned to her post out front as the young man walked the next family through the very same steps.

"Check-in went smoothly. As we strolled toward the pathway that led us to our room, we noticed a traditional island band playing on the far side of the lobby. We walked that direction and came across a young lady with a cart.

The cart jingled as she came to a stop."

"What was on the cart?" asked Bob.

"Pins," answered Kalibar.

"'Hello. Here at Disney, we have a tradition called pin trading. I will give each of you this pin holder that you wear around your neck like this,' she said, showing her ribbon of material, sporting pins on every square inch. She looked to my wife for permission before draping one around my daughter's neck.

She smiled, leaned in low, and whispered to my daughter, 'I'll tell you a secret.' My child's face lit up. 'Everyone that works in the whole place has to trade any pin they have for any one you want to trade.'

"'Any pin I want?' my daughter repeated in awe, drunk with power that surpassed her own parents.

"'Yes, and I am going to start you off with one pin and the holder for free.' She bent low again and said, 'If you ask really nice and smile, I'll bet you can get Dad to give you his pin to trade for the first one you see that you like.'
"She was right, of course. Mine was the first pin sacrificed to my five year-old's newfound pin-trading power.

By then we had forgotten about the band and, instead, headed to our room. On the way, we noticed the Grand Pool and a two story-high slide designed to look like a volcano. My daughter made us promise to bring her back later in the week.

"The next morning, we made our first scheduled stop—breakfast with the Disney characters. I expected this to be little more than characters wandering around at some point during the breakfast hour so that visitors could take a few pictures, but that wasn't the case.

"After we were seated, a waitress in island wear brought us fresh fruit and took our orders. While we waited for our breakfast to arrive, we chatted lightly with some of the other guests and discussed our plans for later in the day.

Suddenly there was a loud crash, a sound that would generally signal a serious delay in your meal.

"I turned to see the commotion and saw Goofy barreling through the prearranged trays, knocking them everywhere. Following him were the only slightly more graceful chipmunks, Chip and Dale. They began visiting each table, posing for pictures and signing autographs.

"I finally got to ask the age-old question: if Mickey is a mouse, Donald is a duck, and Pluto is a dog, then what is Goofy?
"Goofy shook his head knowingly and wrote in my daughter's autograph book: '½ human, ½ dog.'

A mystery of the ages solved.

"Our meal was then served, and as we dined, the three characters continued visiting with the guests. Just as we were finishing our meal, Goofy made another signature entrance, this time carrying an impossible number of brooms and coconuts.

The mayhem that ensued was called the coconut race. Goofy, Chip, and Dale gathered all the children, armed them each with a broom, and set them loose on the coconuts. Delighted laughter filled the air as children pushed coconuts around the dining room.

Somehow the characters managed to fall behind the children at just the right moments to make sure they won the race.

My daughter was delighted at every turn and still remembers it fondly a year later.

"The fun did not stop at breakfast; let me tell you about the rides. They are for the most part just like the rides at any amusement park. Do you remember the airplane ride, the one where the planes are connected to a pole in the center, and you move up and down and around in a circle?

Take the same ride and replace the airplane with Dumbo, and you have created a much more memorable event because the child ties it into the memories of the movie."

"What if you did not like Dumbo?" Bob asked.
"Well, you're in luck. Just a few hundred yards away, the same ride, with minor cosmetic changes and a height-adjusting lever, becomes a flying carpet a la *Aladdin*.

Everything in the entire complex—shuttle buses, hotels, themed rides, shops, and restaurants—is constructed to create memorable experiences far beyond transportation, sleeping, riding, shopping, and eating.

It is the experience that allows Disney to charge premium prices for what is substantively no different from any other amusement park."

"I can see the idea. It's all about making it special enough to remember," said Bob.

"Yes," answered Kalibar. "Make it memorable."

Notes

Chapter 9
The End ... and Beginning

"I hope that the information we have shared with you will be helpful," said Kalibar.

"I am sure it will," answered Bob. "It has given me a great deal to think about on my trip home."

"I've put together some additional information for you." Kalibar handed Bob a small binder. "Thank you for coming. Good luck."

"Thank you," replied Bob, "for opening my eyes to a whole new way of looking at things."

Kalibar smiled his infectious grin, walked Bob to the door of his office, and bid him good-bye.

As Bob walked toward the exit, he glanced first at the Space Invaders game and then to Jessica. She smiled slightly as Bob set his luggage down and pressed the single player button on the old arcade game.

Bob was well into the second level of the game—he was much better at fending off space invaders than he'd remembered—when he was momentarily distracted by the arrival of a flustered-looking man who bustled into the building, luggage in hand.

"You must be Franklin! Welcome to Shinobi Enterprises. My name is Jessica," "Just leave your bags right here. We will look after them while you meet with Mr. Kalibar.

"You are a few minutes early. Please feel free to have a look around, and if you need to check your e-mail or fax something to your office, please use any of our resources," she said, motioning to the black desk.

"One more thing—no quarters needed," she said with a slight grin that this time Bob shared and understood.

Later, as Bob settled into his seat for the flight home and opened the binder from Kalibar, he was not surprised at the question he read on the first page.

Notes

Chapter 10
Why the Experience?

Why the Experience? Because it's not optional!

We may think the Experience is only for Starbucks or Disney. Instead, we have to apply them to Hewlett-Packard, General Motors, and Shell Oil Company. (1) You can add your business to that list, too, provided you are interested in growing, making a profit and embrace the Experience.

Most of us are in business to make a profit. It sounds simple enough.

Let's look at another simple truth. The way to make a profit is to sell something for more than you paid for it. Basically, profit is your selling price minus your cost and overhead.

Let's talk about what we can and cannot control. You can shop around for the items or materials used in your service to get the best price, but your choices are limited by your desired level of quality you must insist on.

 The same is true of your people and workspace. To maintain the highest standards, you must hire the best people. Those people need to have a workspace that allows them to reach their full potential. You would not expect an artist to create a masterpiece in a gray-walled cubical.

Allow your employees the freedom and space that inspires them to create their own masterpiece, be it a spreadsheet or advertising copy.

If you entertain or invite clients into your office, the space becomes even more valuable and will likely be priced accordingly.

Since you cannot drastically change the cost of your inventory or materials, and assuming you have already gotten a great deal on your overhead, that leaves only the price you charge in your control.

Any economist would tell you that market forces largely control the prices you can charge. If you still believe that clients will use your product or service based on the price you charge, remember this marketing truth: someone will always beat your price, and when he or she does, you will lose customers based on that lower price.

I wholeheartedly agree with both the economist and that marketing truth, but you have the ability to change what you sell without retooling a single assembly line or adding a new department.

I am talking about creating an experience, of course. The Experience is the highest of the four levels of an offering: commodities, goods, services, and experiences.*(2)*

A true commodity is bought and sold, generally by the ton. Commodities are raw materials, such as wheat and corn, precious metals, gold and silver, rubber and cotton.

We will use cotton as our example. Though the price of one ton of raw cotton fluctuates daily, let's say that two yards of the combed and processed material sells for five cents. We will assume it takes two yards to make a white undershirt.

Three T-shirts require six yards of cotton material.
Once sewn into a T-shirt, the commodity has now become a good. The cost of the material was fifteen cents, but you will gladly pay $5.99 at Wal-Mart for a three-pack of white T-shirts.

Thus far, the perceived value has increased forty fold from the fifteen cents that the material cost to the purchase price of $5.99, or $2 per shirt, with the change from commodity to good.

The next level of an offering is the service. If we take the same amount of cotton in our three-pack, put it into just one thicker, sturdier shirt, and add five cents worth of black dye, it would bring our cost of production to twenty cents a shirt.

What happens to the perceived value and the selling price? For the service of thickening the cotton and adding a color, we will pay $9.99 for a single shirt. Now we have gone from a fifteen-cent commodity, to a $2 good, to a $9.99 serviced item that is sixty-seven times more than the cost of the original commodity.

Let's take the same black shirt and add the ominous face of Darth Vader from *Star Wars* or Kyle Petty's red number 8 race car, and the perceived value and selling price doubles to $20. That is 133 times the commodity cost.

Why are we suddenly willing to pay so much more for essentially the same item, with an image printed on it? The answer is the same, whether the image depicts a scene from a movie or portrays a sports team or a popular saying—because it reminds us of things we enjoy.

It harkens back to something we loved. When I was growing up, I desperately wanted to be the *Star Wars* character Luke Skywalker, with his light saber and the power of the mystical Force.

Alas, I had not been able to do the things he had done, but because my mother paid 133 times the price of the commodity, I was able to wear his image emblazoned on my T-shirt.

That shirt attached me, albeit distantly, to the experience of a movie that I loved. The depth and closeness of the experience can increase the perceived value and the selling price as well.

Anyone who has ever paid $35 for a T-shirt at a rock concert knows that to be true. Why were we willing to pay 233 times the cost of a commodity to wear a Guns N' Roses shirt?

Because we were there, we were immersed in the sights and sounds.

It is directly linked to our experience at that time. Our experience was shared with thousands of like-minded people. It was filled with the energy that only a live performance could bring. In short, it was a powerful, memorable experience, and that shirt was a reminder of that experience.

Let's review the value of each of the stages of offering of cotton:
Cotton the commodity—15¢
Cotton the (good) undershirt—$2
Cotton the (serviced) colored shirt—$9.99

Those increases are certainly substantial, but when we enter the realm of experience, the value skyrockets:

Cotton the themed shirt—$20
Cotton the themed shirt at a concert or convention—$35

As you can see, the greater the experience, the higher the perceived value and selling price. You may be thinking, "That's fine for a T-shirt, but what about a business?"

Think of an office you have walked into that seemed cold and sterile. No matter how elaborate the decor, if you were not warmly greeted or, in some cases, even acknowledged, the experience probably left you wanting.

That first impression, perhaps subconsciously, affected the entirety of the meeting or purpose of your visit.

On the opposite end of the spectrum, when you've entered a more modest but appropriately decorated office, and were greeted and offered coffee or water, you were most likely put at ease and, again, perhaps without knowing it, your visit was affected in a positive way.

These settings roughly demonstrate the difference between a commodity and an experience. Which would you prefer to sell?

Notes

Chapter 11
Make It Memorable

If I had to boil the whole concept of what creating an experience means to one impossibly short phrase, it would be,

"Make it memorable."

In other words, an experience is something worth remembering.

People can tell you what they wore and what they ate at the dinner when they proposed to their spouse.

Why, then, can they not tell you what they ate or wore three days ago?

Obviously the proposal dinner is one of the most important moments of their life, so they recall it in great detail. It is worth remembering. So how do you make something people might think of as mundane, like your product or service, memorable? That will be the focus of the remainder of the book.

First, you must decide if the experience you are going to create is a "real fake" or a "fake fake" … or is it real?

Notes

Chapter 12
Fake Fakes, Real Fakes, and Reals

The realness or fakeness of an experience has more to do with how it is staged than the topic of the experience itself.

Let's start with a look at fake fakes and real fakes.

The Rainforest Cafe, a tropical rain forest–themed restaurant and retail shop, is an example of a real fake. It has plunging waterfalls, live tropical fish, flashing lightning in manmade mist, and simulated animals growling and roaring from the thick bush that covers walls and accents every table.

But it does not try and convince you that you are actually in a rain forest. Rather, it wants you to experience The Rainforest Cafe.
The key to a real fake is that they use elements of other places, environments, even times, to create an experience that is uniquely their own.

Chick-fil-A is a quick service restaurant; it does everything it can to avoid being called a fast-food restaurant. It has cafe-style tables and cushioned chairs that are not bolted to the floor. Hiring is generally handled by the owner to ensure that the cream of the crop is selected. This provides a casual dining level of service.

The award-winning food is far better than your average fast food joint, primarily because everything is prepared in the restaurant.

You may be surprised to learn that in a quick service restaurant, where most food comes precooked only to be heated in oil, that at Chick-fil-A, hundreds of lemons are squeezed daily for the lemonade served there.

Equally surprising is that the carrots, cabbage, and everything else they use in sides and salads are chopped, cut, and otherwise prepared there daily.

The far-above-average counter service is enhanced by a hostess and a roving, seven-foot-tall cow wearing a sign that reads "Eat Mor Chikin."

The cow can be seen at some restaurants during peak hours to delight the kids.

Chick-fil-A is not trying to convince you that you are in a casual dining restaurant, but rather create an experience that is uniquely Chick-fil-A.

So a real fake is just an experience that may be designed to remind you of something else—a rain forest or casual dining restaurant—but not try to convince you it is the genuine article.

James Gilmore and Joseph Pine, authors of *The Experience Economy*, an excellent book on "the Experience," chose Disney as the perfect example of a fake fake.

"It is not designed to remind you of anything other than what it is—a chance to live the movies you loved as kids and again as adults with your children.

In Disney you never see the teenager in the mouse suit or the machines that move Ariel the mermaid's tail. Nothing looks fake—created, yes, but not fake. Disney World is not a copy of anything. It is a thing."

A traveling Renaissance fair comes through Texas every October and November. It is another example of a fake fake.
The fair obviously is not thirteenth-century England, but everything mundane is hidden. The food vendor cries, "Me lords and ladies! Get your [food item] here!" Steak on a stick is my personal favorite at the fair.

All the prices are marked in "pounds," which are equivalent to U.S. dollars. Even sodas served in plastic bottles are hidden behind screens until handed to the patrons.

Magic shows, juggling acts, and Shakespearean plays are presented on stages that are carefully arranged as not to show that they are simply facades.

Even the parking row signs are shield-shaped and written in Old English script.

Again, it is not an attempt to really be the thirteenth century but to be a real Renaissance fair.

That leaves the reals. A "real" experience, at first glance, seems to be the purview of nature with such magnificence of the Grand Canyon, the Painted Desert, and the massive redwoods in northern California.

But in reality, it is where your service business may need to be in a manner of speaking, all experiences are real because they involve real people, real time, and real things, but for the purpose of this explanation, "real" will be an experience that is what it appears to be.

The Potato Patch, where Nicole had lunch every Tuesday, for example, was a restaurant that specialized in down-home Southern taste and hospitality.

The food was prepared in accordance with that theme. The hostess greeted customers in a welcoming manner, the wait staff treated everyone like family, and the roll-throwing guys were just like the brothers one might have gotten in trouble with for throwing food at the table. It did not seek to remind customers of anything or to tie into any previous memories. It was just what it appeared to be—a country-style restaurant with particularly good chicken fried steak. In short, it was real.

Shinobi presents a real experience; at Shinobi Enterprises Incorporated, we produce the experience of our stated goal, which is creating outrageously great marketing strategies and training programs.

To that end, everything from the less-than–normal design of the building, the gym, flex lunches, even the Space Invaders arcade game, are all in place to provide a creative, nontraditional, out-of-the-box environment to aid in creating outrageously great ideas for our clients.

Jessica greets clients, current and prospective, as they enter the office to make them feel as welcome and comfortable as possible.

The more at ease a client is, the greater the information flow he or she is able to give. The more information we have, the better the concepts we can create. The variety of people and the freedoms they enjoy at work ensure that varied and multifaceted ideas make up the basis of our goal of creating outrageously great ideas for our clients.

Notes

Chapter 13
Four Out of Five Senses Agree

We all observe and experience the world through our senses. We hear and see thousands of messages every day. How do you create an experience that goes beyond the clutter to reach the all-important memorable experience level?

Engage more senses.

A fine restaurant has the luxury of being able to engage each sense directly.

At Chez Pierre, the decor was wonderful, the seats plush, and the music from a live harp unique and beautiful. The aroma from the kitchen was matched only by the taste of the exquisite dinner prepared by the incredibly skilled chef.

There are obviously situations that do not allow you to engage all the senses, particularly taste and smell.

Remember to think about what experience you are trying to put on or stage. Let me give you an example. A Realtor was talking strategies to a home seller. The first suggestions were the obvious things—keep the house immaculate, leave the pets in the backyard, and have the family out of the house during showings.

The next idea puzzled the seller. The Realtor suggested that she bake a batch of cookies just before a prospective buyer looked at the house.

The Realtor explained that the smell of freshly baked cookies would conjure images of family and friends sharing those warm cookies around the kitchen table with a glass of cold milk and great conversation.

The potential buyer would connect with an experience that had nothing to do with the house itself, but rather with the prospect of an enjoyable event that could happen there.

When a buyer is looking at five houses in ninety minutes the created experience certainly makes the one house more memorable than the others.

In real estate, being memorable is the name of the game.

If you take time to look at offices that you visit, you may see things like potpourri or scented candles in waiting areas and hear the soothing sounds of classical music wafting gently through. These atmosphere-enhancing props certainly do not make the lawyer whose office you're in any better.

They do, however, make your wait more pleasant and create a more welcoming experience.

The more senses you can engage in a pleasant way, the greater chance you have of creating a memorable experience.

Notes

Chapter 14
The Four Realms of Experience

So you have decided to create a memorable experience by engaging all the senses. You have chosen among fake fake, real fake, and real experiences.

 Now you must choose how the participant will interact with your experience.

Pine and Gilmore have created "Four Realms of Experience," based on the level of participation, from passive to active, and the level of involvement, from simply absorbing the event to being immersed in it.*(2)*

 I will give a brief explanation of each and how it applies to the traveling Renaissance festival.

The most common of staged events is **entertainment.** It is observed through touch, sight, sound, and, in some cases, even taste and smell.

It is on the light side of both the participation and involvement scale. Watching a play or television and reading for pleasure are examples of **entertainment**.

Some experiences allow participants to choose which realm of experience they prefer.

The Texas Renaissance Festival is one such experience. If a patron wants to remain in the **entertainment** realm, there are a variety of shows throughout the fairgrounds.

Additionally, there are roving minstrels and acting groups that personalize their acts for the audiences, in hopes of receiving a handsome tip, of course.

Let's say a participant wants to move up the involvement scale, the next level would be the **educational** experience.

In an **educational** experience, a participant absorbs the things happening before him while actively participating in the events.

The guest is now actively participating in the event. It could be as basic as observing in hopes of repeating the process at a later time.

Others may be physically involved, such as with dancing or sports training. Back at the Renaissance Festival, for those who seek the educational experience, glass-blowing demonstrations, as well as classes for boot-making, basket-crafting, and other skills are available.

In each case, the key is a higher level of involvement.

My personal favorite is the **escapist** experience. In an **escapist** experience, the person actively participates in the event while immersing himself in the environment.

The **escapist** is at the maximum on both the involvement and participation scale. These are people who love casinos, volunteering at magic shows, or any place where they can be a part of the action while being surrounded by the sight, sounds, and even the smell of the event itself.

The Renaissance Festival provides for the escapist by catering to their need to have all of senses engulfed by the experience. The more senses engaged, the deeper, richer, and—most importantly—more memorable the experience becomes.

Escapists attend the Renaissance Festival in full costume, often rivaling the paid performers. They want other patrons to mistake them for performers in the festival itself.

Some dress in costume to further immerse themselves into the environment; a popular notion among patrons that actually became a financial opportunity for the festival.

To capitalize on that need, the festival now rents costumes to those inclined to dress the part.

Escapists find a way to become a part of the show. They interact with other patrons and the many shopkeepers. Savvy shopkeepers know that having a performer in their shop increases the experience for their prospective customers.

The **escapists** become part of the experience for others, which creates a much richer, more memorable experience for themselves as well.

The **aesthete** is the escapist's friend that came with him but did not dress up.

With an **aesthetic** experience, individuals immerse themselves but do not become directly involved. The aesthete takes a step down the participation scale but remains highly immersed.

Sitting in a French cafe, standing amid the great redwoods, or gazing at Mount Rushmore, one cannot help but be immersed in the sight and sound of such wonders. But how does one participate in such things? You do not.

You are simply there.

The **aesthete** that joins his more gregarious friend at the Renaissance Festival has no desire to play a part but is happy to be totally immersed as the events unfold around him.

When you choose what experience you are staging, choose carefully the realm or realms of experience you wish to create. You may find that what you create may offer something to the aesthete, the escapist, and the education and entertainment seekers.

Notes

Chapter 15
What Ties it Together?

We have talked about many aspects of the Experience. Now come the big questions. How do you stage an experience? Where do you begin?

What do The Potato Patch, Renaissance Festival, Rainforest Cafe, and Shinobi Enterprises all have in common? A theme. A well thought out, purposely developed theme by which all aspects of the experience are selected.

Your theme will influence your decor, letterheads, employee choices, and even clients.

The Potato Patch had the down-home Southern home cooking theme. To that end, the name of the restaurant, the menu choices, and the Texas sweet tea in the huge glasses all work to reinforce that theme.

The motto for The Rainforest Cafe is "It's a Wild Place to Eat and Shop." A simulated rain forest is only the beginning of the lengths that it goes to create and bolster that theme. From the entrance, where you find carnival-style games, to the fiery, sparkling volcano dessert, everything is created around their theme to make you believe that you are in a 'Wild Place to Eat and Shop.'

That's all fine and good for themed restaurants, you might say, but what about a serious business?

At Shinobi Enterprises, we have a theme as well: to craft incredible experiences and outrageously good marketing strategies. Let's look at how that affects the creation and daily running of the business.

First, any business is only as good as its people. To meet the stated theme, I must hire people that have all of the basic qualifications of the position. Beyond that, they must be creative, just a little unusual, and have the ability to work in a less-than-traditional atmosphere.

I want my people always to be at the top of their game and able to give our clients and each other their very best. With that in mind, I provide a workout area, flex scheduling, and opportunities to attend seminars pertinent not only to their work life, but also to their personal development.

We discourage work on Saturday, and give everyone Sundays off to worship or spend time with family and relax. The better employees feel—physically, mentally, and spiritually—the better they will perform.

These great employees could not be expected to create incredible experiences and outrageously good marketing in a traditional, gray-walled, cubical-filled office environment.

The uniqueness of the lobby that greets them every morning and the freedom to create a personal office space, whether it is slightly outlandish or completely traditional, continue to support the theme.

Even client selection is influenced by the theme. In fact, it is the area most influenced. A client that is instantly turned off by the slight uniqueness of the decor, or a client that cannot believe a professional office could ever include a Space Invaders game or a collection of action figures, would most likely not accept the out-of-the box, creative approach to building experiences and the great marketing that we produce.

As you can see, everything, from employees to office space to clients, is created and chosen in accordance with the stated theme.

So, now that you understand the themes of The Potato Patch, Renaissance Festival, The Rainforest Cafe, and Shinobi Enterprises, what should your theme be?
Be cautious not to confuse goals with themes.

For example, being one of the top three CPA firms in the Dallas area is not a theme. It is a worthwhile long-term goal, but it lacks the components that make a theme worth the paper it's written on.

A theme must be specific.

A general theme, like a general goal, does not provide a clear direction; it is paramount that anyone reading your theme will instantly understand what you are trying to accomplish. It needs to have an emotional component, and it has to give direction to everyone who reads it.

The emotional component is so important because people chose to follow or buy something, anything emotionally and then justify it logically. No matter how well thought out and academically sound your theme is, if your people are not 100% behind it your clients will never experience it.

A client actually presented me with this theme. I responded by asking her what she thought it would take to become one of the top three firms in Dallas.

She quickly answered that the first and most important thing was to be accurate.

 Secondly, she said, we must be easy to get in contact with and responsive to clients' questions. Other issues certainly emerged, but because these were the two most significant, I suggested the following theme: "XYZ CPAs is the most accurate and friendly firm in the Dallas area."

How would this theme affect the running of the firm? A prudent manager would hire the candidate with a personality that reflects the firm's theme. Indeed, the manager may even overlook a stern mannered candidate with more qualifications in favor of the candidate with a friendlier demeanor with acceptable qualifications.

The manner in which clients are greeted and how much time they spend in the waiting room would be changed to include more personal attention and shorter waits. You would not keep a friend standing outside on your porch all day while you finished a phone call. Should you be any less considerate of a client?

The type of clients the firm attracts would be changed as well. We all know the old sayings "Birds of a feather flock together" and "Like attracts like." The result of making accuracy and friendliness the key elements of the theme ensures two things. First, "accuracy" meets the requirement of the professional relationship of a CPA firm. Meeting the basic requirements must always be the most important part of any theme.

Secondly, when "friendliness" is part of the theme, it becomes a core belief and will attract like-minded clients.

A firm's theme is the framework by which all decisions are made. Any action being considered can by tested by asking the following question: will this action uphold, if not further, the founding principles of the company's theme? If the answer is anything but a resounding yes, the action should be given much more serious consideration before it is implemented. A company's theme becomes its guiding light.

Good luck, Bob. I hope your time with us here at Shinobi Enterprises was everything you had expected it to be and a little more. If there is anything else we can do to help, please feel free contact us.

Notes

Chapter 16
You're Up

Let's recap the key points. In creating your own theme, remember to carefully consider what you really want your company to be. Remember that the theme will act as a framework for every decision you make for your business.

It must be specific, and it needs to have an emotional component.
Do not confuse goals with themes. To be the top law office in your city is a worthwhile goal, but it does not offer clients or employees any direction.

Plus, subjective terms such as "top" can have radically different meanings to different people. For example, a potential client might understand that to mean the top-grossing firm and take his business to someone he perceives as not in it for the money.

From within the company, an employee might take top to mean that small clients should be overlooked in an effort to gain only top-tier clients.

A better theme for a law office might be "Bringing our expertise to solve your issues in plain English."

That theme states that the law office will have experts to work on your legal issues and that they will do so in a way that you can understand. It sends a clear message to associates and clients alike.

You're up.

Take some time to carefully choose your theme. Once you have come up with a few solid ideas, employ feedback from your key staff to shape the final form.

After all, they will be the ones carrying forward your ideals. You want to ensure their belief in the company's image.

I want your theme to be inspired. Take some time in a quiet place, think of what you love about your business, and jot them down. What are the things that are most important to your clients, list those as well. If the two lists have a few things in common you very likely have the beginning of your theme.

I have given you the information, and you were motivated enough to read this book. Now create that inspired theme.

You have it? Great! Now go back to chapter 10, and record how each chapter plays into your theme. Will the experience created around this theme be a "real fake" (like The Rainforest Café), a "fake fake" (like the Renaissance Festival) or "real" (like seeing the Grand Canyon).

What senses can you engage? Be creative on this one, and remember the fresh baked cookies engaged the sense of smell, a sense generally overlooked to entice potential house buyers.
Will you create your experience to entertain, to educate, or to appeal to the aesthete or escapist?

Although Bob and his particular visit were fabricated, the advice offered by Kalibar is as genuine as it is timeless. I hope that what you've read here will inspire you to create your own experiences.

Thank you for joining Bob and I on this journey. I hope it has been an experience you will not soon forget.

Good luck, and may you discover the power of "The Experience"!

As always, may you achieve success as you define it!

Chapter 17

Articles

The New Rule of Three

Have you ever been overwhelmed by the enormity of a task you were given? Confused by the numerous aspects of a complex assignment? Do complicated situations demand complicated responses? I say the answer is as simple as 3, The Rule of Three.

The Rule of Three introduced itself to me in too many aspects of my life to ignore the application in today's business world. The first time I recall hearing The Rule of Three, although it was not named as such, was in the military. "When confronting and enemy," the gnarled old sergeant said, "how many sides do you want to attack from?" A room full of young Airman unanimously concluded that attacking from all four sides was the correct answer. The old sergeant shook his head and asked the simple question, "If you are trapped by the enemy what would you do?" Fight to the last man, we agreed. Now the sergeant said, "If you attack from three sides, you give the enemy a place to go." He headed off further questions by adding,"You control where they go, most likely into a position where they will be attacked from three sides."

The Rule of Three again made itself known to me in martial arts training. My instructor said "You can overcome a larger, stronger opponent if you have solid technique and control timing, distance, and emotion." In martial arts, controlling distance and timing is accomplished by where you place yourself using distance, and the angle in which you face your opponent. Being at an odd distance and angle, you force your opponent to constantly adjust breaking his rhythm, timing, and overall effectiveness. You begin controlling emotions with your own; you master your fear or excitement to reach a state of calm. From a place of calm you can taunt your opponent to anger him and keep him off balance; you can try and reason with them, or even stroke their ego to the point that the fight is no longer necessary in their mind.

During a recent marketing campaign I began researching what successful businesses had in common. There were many things, but I should not have been surprised when three main topics surfaced again and again.

It was then that I named the phenomenon: The New Rule of Three. Simply put, when you identify the three most important factors in virtually any endeavor and concentrate on them, the majority of other smaller factors will fall into place.

The Rule of Three seemed to hold firm in business as it had in virtually every aspect of life. I set out to decide how best to help people succeed. I had to decide what the major factors of success in business were…

> ➤ Leadership (yours)
> ➤ Talent (in your people)
> ➤ Marketing…
> …are the three in The Rule of Three for today's business.

Let's examine each in brief. First your leadership, as an owner or top-level manager you must give clear instructions, you must set a course for employees to follow. There is quite a bit to leadership you might say. I agree. But leadership itself is key. I teach a workshop on leadership to CEO's and top tier managers. The three major components are direction, communication and motivation. These three actions, or actionable goals, set the stage for great leadership.

A leader must have and share the direction for their company and employees; they are the captain of the ship. For anyone to communicate a direction they must know a few things. First, they must know what they actually want out of life. This is called a Personal Vision, which is a written explanation of a scene some years in the future explaining what the leader wants his life to look like in say 10 years. If in the vision he is spending 4 days a week with his family he should begin to train someone to take over a large portion of his daily activities. If the vision dictates passing the business on to her child there are a host of actions that she should begin to implement. As the name suggests a Personal Vision is shared with a precious few, but it should greatly affect everything the leader does in their planning.

Secondly a leader must have a Public Vision. The vision is not fluff, but again a picture of where the leader wants to take the business in a set amount of time. It should be include the scope you will achieve, will you be known, statewide, nationally even globally. What will you be known for? Who will you help and how will you help them in the process. The Public Vision is shared with staff, vendors, customers everyone associated with the business. It is an inspiration and realistic picture of what is to come for the business.

With these to vision well in hand the leader must create a Strategic Plan. Planning need not be complicated or as stressful as it is often thought of. Simply take the three parts of your Public Vision and ask what must happen for these things to occur. These will be your over arcing goals. For each over arching goal, chose three strategies that will lead to its coming to fruition. Find for these strategies the three actions that must be taken for the completion of that strategy. It is a simple cause and effect. If the actions are taken, then the strategies will be executed, and with the completion of the strategies the over arcing goals will be realized.

The formula holds true no matter the complexity of the objective, you may need more layers, but so long as you create an actionable goal with the higher strategy in mind you will achieve success. The simplicity of this planning method is perfect for accountability. Every goal and strategy can be given to a person or department with a time table. The actionable goal demands a definitive answer to the question was this completed and when. It leaves no confusion as to who is responsible for each goal and allows for direct correction or celebration as warranted.

That CEO with a great plan that does not or cannot communicate that plan to his people will not have the support or buy-in that it takes to make the plan the profitable reality it could be. If the plan is communicated effectively and no one cares, it is equally doomed. People that are motivated will give a well-communicated plan the benefit of the doubt and begin implementing their task in the larger context of the overall plan.

Celebration of a well-done task and effective completion of their aspect of the plan will keep staff working hard. The celebration becomes motivation, which breeds good work habits that lead to task completion and quality work leading to celebration. The cycle continues to build on itself until everyone is incredibly motivated all the time. We all know the higher the motivation the greater the productivity.

The celebration need not be expensive or time-consuming. A thank you note written, not emailed, to the employee and the employee's boss or their bosses' boss, will have a drastic effect on moral. Throw out the old employee of the month plaque, $100 bonus, and parking space, and instead personalize a gift. A pair of Texans tickets to a sports fan or a subscription to Canoeing Today for the outdoor type will have a much great impact and in some cases may be less expensive.

Using The Rule of Three we have broken leadership down into three actionable goals: direction, communication and motivation. These goals are easily set and with simple follow-through will have the desired effect of Leadership, in short the organization accomplishing the vision of the leaders and having a great time doing it.

Secondly, as Jim Collins points out in *Good to Great* the right people are critically important to a company's growth and success. I named talent as the second in The Rule of Three for today's business. As you might imagine I have three actionable items here as well.

First, chose the right people with the right talent. I am amazed that people would hire someone to head a department that represents 30% of their revenue, be that $10,000 or $10 million, but will not spend the relatively small amount of money on background checks or time doing a thorough check of references.

A client of mine confided in me that he had gone through over 100 applications and many interviews and had hired only two people. You might be thinking he must have been hiring for a CFO or other very important position. You would be right - he was hiring for the front counter of his quick service restaurant. The cashiers are the hands and face of his business. By the way he and the chain of which he is a part have been locally and nationally recognized for superior customer service for the last 13 years.

Secondly, well-trained talent (people) will maximize productivity as well. When I was an employee my boss sent me to the Franklin Covey Time Management course. It was certainly an investment for him, the better use I made of my time the more I produced for him. A secondary benefit was a feeling motivation at being given the opportunity to better myself. A few years ago after turning that employer into my first client, I took his entire management staff to a Zig Ziglar motivational seminar.

The last key to keeping great talent can be found on every list ever published on the subject of "Why do people leave a job?" The number one answer is always "feeling unappreciated." In some extreme cases, not feeling acknowledged at all. As a leader you should be in a constant cycle of communicating with and motivating and celebrating your talent's productivity. If you follow that model your people will never feel unappreciated.

Your thee actionable goals for the second component in The Rule of Three, Talent, are pick the right people, keep their skills and knowledge current, and show your appreciation.

These three activities will drastically improve the implementation of your vision and the plans created from it and will insure the greatest opportunity for success.

Lastly, you must get the message about your great products and services to your best prospects. In other words…Marketing.

Marketing holds a special place for me as it was what started me in business; I learned early on that marketing had three distinct parts, the message, the target market, and the distribution method. The best crafted message that is delivered to the wrong people will yield nothing. Of course a great message, intended for the right target that is never received due to poor placement, is equally worthless.

The right message is different for every business, but it must include your unique selling proposition; in short it must say what you do better, faster, or cheaper than everyone else. It should be completely honest and have a call to action and all the possible ways prospects can find or get in touch with you, phone number, email, apps and your website. If you have gotten their attention, make sure it is easy for them to buy from you.

Once you have crafted you message, you must carefully chose the target market you wish to reach. We all know that the top 20% of our clients provide us with 80% of our business, hence the 80/20 rule. I submit that you create a profile from only your top 20%. You chose how you define the top 20% - highest revenue, easiest to work with, however you define them. Once you know who they are, find out where they work, live, and play. Armed with that knowledge, you can determine the most productive distribution method, marketing to only those that fit the profile of your top 20%.

Any marketing campaign worth its salt will use different methods of getting the message to the intended prospects. Some of the most common are radio, television, direct mail, ad placement, and the often misused and maligned couponing. The key to great distribution is staying focused. Once you have identified your target market you can select billboards in a small area most frequented by your prospects or place ads in children's magazines or have entries in holiday parades if your target is families in a certain geographic area.

Cable channels have made television advertising much more affordable and easier to focus by allowing you to select not only geographical area but the ability to purchase ads in programs tailored to the interest you identified as your target market.

There are many methods and each business should explore many and test a few. Once you find those that effectively reach your focused target market, use them consistently, tweaking the message and offers to keep them fresh and you will have effective marketing

The implementation of The Rule of Three in business today, Leadership, Talent, and Marketing, can simplify the complex and put straightforward actionable goals with great results easily within your reach.

May you achieve success as you define it!

David Whitfield

Marketing and Business Dynamics

PO Box 1603

Cypress, TX 77410

DavidWhitfield@TheNewRuleofThree.com

www.TheNewRuleofThree.com

Friday September 24 and October 1, 2004
The DCR Houston's Daily Business Newspaper
One Minute Marketer

Words Mean Things

Well of course they do, that's what they do, they mean stuff . The question is which words mean which stuff . Rush Limbaugh is often heard saying he possesses "talent on loan from God." A well-meaning caller suggested that God had given him that talent. Limbaugh, using only the title of this tip as explanation, assured her that he meant what he said: "On loan from God."

The caller was attempting to pay him a compliment, but Limbaugh was making the point that his talent was beyond mere mortal ability and therefore was simply being borrowed from on high.

 You do not have to agree with Limbaugh's politics, but he is certainly a successful wordsmith. I am not sure I agree with the statement about his talent, but I am sure Words Mean Things.
Join me next Friday and learn the difference between a client and a customer, and what it can mean to your bottom line.

You may have noticed the word customer rarely, if ever, appears in my writings. Customer is defined by Webster's as "one that purchases some commodity or service.

" Whereas, a client is defined as "a person who engages
the professional advice or services of another." My question is simple: which would you like to be considered, a client or a customer? A restaurant for which I consult recently changed all instances of the word customer to guest, in everything from the annual plan to the Employee Training and Policies Manual. If you think these changes are purely semantics, I believe you are mistaken.

If a restaurant staff thinks of you as a guest, they will treat you very differently than as merely "one that purchases a commodity."

Instill in everyone in your company the idea that you do not have customers, but instead clients, guests, or partners, and you will see a far-reaching, profit-generating change in the service your clients receive.

October 4th and 5th 2004
The DCR Houston's Daily Business Newspaper
One Minute Marketer

Get Specific

Get specific. Have you ever sat back and thought about what you would do if you won the lottery? Ah…dreams - they are great for the lottery, not so good for marketing plans and strategies.

Most often, when you ask someone or yourself what your marketing plans are, you may list several ideas. "We are beefing up our customer service," "I think direct mail is promising," and many other thoughts. All of those thoughts are just about as good for something as the lottery dream. It is said that goals that are not written down are just dreams.

You plan your expenses in a budget, your strategies in a strategic plan, so marketing that brings in new business deserves the same forethought and attention to detail.

At Marketing and Business Dynamics, we define marketing a little differently than Webster's: we say marketing is "effectively getting your message to your prospects repeatedly." Get specific with your message. If you do not have a firm idea of what your message is, that is the first place to start.

Your marketing message should be whatever it is you do faster, cheaper, more creatively, or better than everyone else. That is known as your competitive edge, your "Unique Selling Proposition" or USP.

Find out what your USP is and make it the centerpiece of your marketing. If you cannot identify your USP, make one - and fast.

Who do I tell? You know your message; that is whatever you do better, faster, cheaper, than everyone else, your "Unique Selling Proposition." So who do you share that message with – who is your target market?

The more precise you can identify your niche within your target market, the better. Consider basing your niche on the top 20% of your current clients. Once you have the group chosen, examine the things they have in common. Be sure to focus on all aspects of the group member's lives; do not limit yourself to their business commonalities.

It is these common traits that likely cause them to need your product or service. You may have to look closely to see any similarities in the group, but rest assured the work will be richly rewarded by the savings a focused marketing effort gives over the traditional shotgun approach.

Go beyond the obvious demographic information such as age, gender, and race. Look for lifestyles and activities that they may share, such a golf, family outings, etc. This information will tell you where your best prospects live, work, and play.

Armed with this information, you can put your message in the media found in those places, where it will be seen repeatedly.

Wednesday September 29, 2004
The DCR Houston's Daily Business Newspaper
Answers from the Board

Appreciation Goes a Long Way Towards Motivation

Dear Board,

I own a ten-person, professional security firm. I have six long-time employees and four newer employees. I want to keep them all motivated, but I have two questions. Do I have to do the same thing for everyone, new and old, and other than big cash bonuses what can I do to motivate them?

Signed,
Wanting happy people

Dear Wanting,

Let's start with what motivation is. According to *Essential Managers Manual* by Heller and Hindle, "motivation is the will to act."

That being the case, your employee's base motivation is the security of their job, the base of the whole Needs Hierarchy from Psychology 101. That base motivation may get them to work every day, but is unlikely to make them the never-ending source of customer pleasing, ever increasing profit driving superstars that you want.

The good news is that big money bonuses do not correlate with job satisfaction, much less motivation. In fact, five out of five articles I researched with titles like "The Top Ten Reasons People Leave a Job" list money issues at number four or below. This phenomenon is not limited to the United States; one of the aforementioned articles came from an Irish business newspaper.

Money is not the answer - so what is? For the answer, we go back to our articles. The top three reasons listed, without fail, come down to a common issue. A failure to feel important, appreciated, respected, or in some extreme cases, acknowledged.

That would be at the top of the Psychology 101hierarchy. People need to feel as if what they do has worth; men in particular derive the majority of their self-worth from their work lives.

Do we give everyone a vice president's title and a key to the newly designated executive washroom? I think not.

Let's take one idea at a time.

To make an employee feel important you must first value their contribution and let them know that. Weekly meetings are a great time to pass out earned recognition awards; people love to hear their names, particularly when the words 'good job' precedes it.

I applaud any company that has a recognition program such as Employee of the Month, etc. The danger is that static programs of that nature turn into popularity contests or are decided based on who has not been selected yet. The parking place and $100 prize are quickly used and forgotten in the rush and grind of daily work and the sameness of the award.

As a small company you have the opportunity to know your employees and have an understanding of what they like on and off the clock. Imagine the impact a subscription to Canoe Monthly would have on the office outdoors fanatic that comes in from the weekend telling everyone about the latest trip down the river.

Likewise the tickets to Sunday's football game given to the office manager that has a Houston Texans Football' flag at her desk.

To motivate your people, make sure when you are handing out praise to do so as often as warranted, or reward them in such a way that shows your employees that you have actually taken the time to know them as well as their work.

Wednesday October 6, 2004
The DCR Houston's Daily Business Newspaper
Answers from the Board

Private, Business Life can be a Balancing Act

Dear Board,

I own a strip center mailbox and shipping business - heck I am the business. I am open Monday through Saturday, 10 a.m. to 6 p.m. My wife helps out sometimes, but it's basically just me. How can I run the business that is just starting to grow and still have some kind of family life?

Signed,
Short on time

Dear Short,

Do not feel like you are alone in this, I am writing this column in my home office at 7:30 p.m. In fact, a recent study of more than 50,000 employees from a variety of manufacturing and service organizations found that, "Two out of every five employees are dissatisfied with the balance between their work and their personal lives," says the study's author, Bruce Katcher, president of the Discovery Group, a management consulting firm.

There are many schools of thought, too many to cover all of them here, but I will give you a few tips that will help.

Set realistic expectations for yourself and your family. You have to be realistic when you plan both your business life and your family life. In your case, as a one-man operation, you have very few options at work other than shorter hours or hiring help.

I encourage you to hire a part-time employee as soon as the business can support one. A few hours two or three nights a week can provide much needed rest and renewal.

Plan, no I mean actually write a plan, for the time you have with your family. The first part of that plan has to be your priorities.

You have to be your first priority; you must take care of yourself first or you will be in no shape to take care of your family or business.

Taking care of yourself includes a few minutes of relaxing before you get home to your family, maybe workouts a few times a week and at least one evening outing that is just for you to have fun and recharge your batteries.

Your second priority has got to be your family. It is your family that you are working for and that will give you the support to help you through the hard times. Set aside time for each member of your family weekly, make sure you have two or three date nights a month with your wife, it will pay off on the nights you have to put in the extra hours.

Plan interactive activities with your children - the kind where you actually talk to each other or read to the younger children. I have sat through a few tea parties in my time and I would not trade anything for those cookies, pretend or otherwise.

Plan your off time with the same care and thoughtfulness you plan your business and you will find following your business plan is easier as well.

Wednesday September 22, 2004
The DCR Houston's Daily Business Newspaper
Answers from the Board

Finding Solutions to the Dreaded Cash Flow Problem

Dear Board,

I have owned an electrical contracting company in Houston, TX for more than 10 years, and I have a strong customer base and good relationships with my vendors. 65% of my business is institutional that I get from general contractors with the rest coming from residential and business service calls. The institutional portion is slow paying and is causing me to have cash flow problems. What options do I have?

Signed,
Sparky

Dear Sparky,
Cash flow is often an issue even when businesses are doing well and especially when a business is starting to pick up after a down time.

There are several possibilities depending on how severe your need is. First, contact your vendors and see if you might increase the payment times and terms for your materials, that will ease your cash flow burden.

Secondly, consider a revolving line of credit or loan at your existing bank or credit union. If the need is extreme, look into factoring; factoring, in short, is selling your accounts receivable for a fee, generally a percentage, to another company that pays you a portion immediately and takes on the burden of collecting from your customers. Insure your profit margins can withstand the fee charged by the factoring firm. You may find it less expensive to take the delayed payment from your customers.

Some customers may not take kindly to their invoices being sold, so consider carefully the best route to take concerning factoring.
In addition to the purely financial methods, there are some long-term possibilities. The business and residential service are generally cash on completion; you can capitalize on this. To insure cash flow does not continue as a problem, consider increasing the percentage of your service business as a

total percentage of revenues. By shifting more of your resources, marketing, and operational, to gaining and servicing additional business and residential service customers, you will create immediate cash flow with every service call you make.

To learn more about factoring, you can contact Eric Standlee Director of Private Funding and Bank Relations at American Prudential Capital, Inc.

Bibliography

(1) Peters, Tom. 2003. *Re-imagine*. London, England: Dorling
Kindersley Limited (page 39)
(2) Joseph Pine II and James H. Gilmore 1999 *The Experience
Economy: Work is Theater & Every Business a Stage*. Boston, Mass.:
Harvard Business School Press (pages 40 and 52)

Recommended Reading

Beckwith, Harry. 1997. Selling the Invisible: A Field Guide to Modern
Marketing. Avenue of the Americas, New York: Warner Books Inc.
Ziglar, Zig. 1997. Over the Top. Nashville, Tenn.: Thomas Nelson, Inc.
Anything by Stephen Covey, Jim Collins and Tom Peters.

About the Author

David Whitfield, as a columnist and reporter for Go Local Magazine, is an experienced writer and a speaker in the fields of marketing, customer service, and business growth. Whitfield lives outside of Houston with his wife and their two daughters.

To learn more or schedule a speaking date or consultation, please visit www.TheNewRuleofThree.com or write:
Shinobi Enterprises Inc.
PO Box 1603
Cypress, TX 77410

Full Biographical information for David Whitfield

David Whitfield is an experienced writer and speaker in Experience Marketing, customer service, strategic planning and business growth.

He is published in Go Local and formerly a business columnist with daily marketing tips in the Daily Court Review.

He has been heard on syndicated Radio, cable and broadcast television and published in The Houston Business Journal, the Houston Chronicle, Your Houston Business Magazine and several other newspapers and newsletters as well as on the Internet. He is the Principle Consultant for the firm he established and has been recognized and awarded for his work in the community and for his excellence in marketing and business.

Whitfield graduated from Cy-Fair High School in Houston, TX in 1987. Upon graduation he joined the United States Air Force serving ten years in England, Japan, South Korea, the United Arab Emirates and the US as a Security Police Officer. In addition to traditional education he has made it his life goal to continue seeking knowledge at every available opportunity. Whitfield has additional training and/or certification in the following areas: Strategic Business Leadership Coaching, Leadership School, Total Quality Management Level 1,2,and 3, The Karrass Effective Negotiating Class, Train the Trainer, Equal Opportunity Employer 2000, and The Franklin Covey Time Management Course (x2).

Whitfield's marketing experience began in the military as the public relations representative for his unit. In addition to serving as the point of contact for all base level Law Enforcement promotions (D.A.R.E., National Night Out etc…), he also became involved in community campaigns (United Way, Blood Drives and US Bond Drives).

Twenty years of entrepreneurship has given him the opportunity to market and consult for many types of businesses including property rentals, Industrial and Corporate firms, Creative Expression Gift Shop, Educational Assistance and many more.

In 1998 Whitfield was contracted as the Marketing Director at a single Chick-fil-A in Houston. Through a combination of media, community involvement, event marketing, and others strategies he increased targeted sales by 50% and overall sales by 18% annually. Just nine months later two additional Chick-fil-A's asked for Whitfield's marketing expertise, which led to his new title as Marketing Director for Central Houston.

The combined the sum of his experience and education lead to the creation of an entrepreneurial marketing style that focuses on low cost, highly effective marketing strategies. These strategies are based on knowledge of a firm's customer and trade area as well as finding and seizing opportunities within those areas. Focused Marketing's slogan explains the company's intention well: Target your best prospect at minimum expense.

The addition of Strategic Success Planning and Targeted Testing International has increased the resources, products and service to a previously unheard of level.

Some of David's awards and Achievements

A Proud Flagship Member of Power in Numbers

A guest Expert and Panelist at the 2010 International Education and Global Entrepreneurship Week

Chosen as Start Up Nation's Spotlight on Success by October 2005

American Entrepreneurs Association: Charter Member

Cy-Fair Chamber of Commerce:
Chairman of the Business in Growth Academy
Chairman of the Networking Breakfast (former)
Chair/Facilitator of Referrals Are Dynamic (former)

Board Member Langham Creek YMCA (former)

Nominated for Cy-Fair Chamber Small Business of The Year 2004 and 2005

Chairman's Award Winner for Cy-Fair Chamber 2001

Chairman of the Cy-Fair Blood Bank Community Promotions Board (former)

White Knight Boys Club: Chairman of Instruction (former)

Delta Epsilon Chi (former)

Thank you for your time and attention, my hope is, as always…

May you find success as You define it!

10167941R00066

Made in the USA
Charleston, SC
12 November 2011